Contents

A fanfare for Monio and Oojilet

I bet you know a bit about Romeo and Juliet – that well-known pair from William Shakespeare's love story. They fell in love, but their families were full of hate. They wed, but their love ended in death by poison and a dagger. A sad story.

But are you aware of the tale of Monio and Oojilet? No? Well, at last their story can be shared...

Monio Montagoo was 29 and did not want to get wed. He had avoided getting ensnared into what he called the "wedding trap" but things were getting a bit hairy at home.

His dad was fairly rich (he had lots of shares and things) and was keen to pair Monio off with Oojilet Carpalot. Her family were very rich. Her mum and dad were so rich they owned a pair of Italian football teams!

Monio always got his own way and most of the time he just cared about himself. He did not care to marry Oojilet. He compared her to a ... no, it would be unfair to repeat it.

And what of the fair Oojilet? She felt the same way about Monio. Mr and Mrs Carpalot agreed with Mr and Mrs Montagoo that their children would make a lovely pair.

In fact, Mr and Mrs Carpalot didn't care who Oojilet married, as long as it happened soon. Oojilet was a nightmare! Her mum and dad were a bit scared of her. She was so spoiled that she was often in a rage and they had to be aware of upsetting their little Princess Hissy Fit (as they called her when they were alone).

Oojilet was soon to be 28, and the Carpalots got a rare smile from her when they agreed to have a party to celebrate. She made them promise that Monio would not be invited.

Barely had Oojilet left the room when her mum rang the Montagoos.

"Yes, a party for sweet Oojilet. Do bring Monio along with you!"

Adults just can't be trusted to keep promises.

But Monio wouldn't go to the party – at least not until Daddy promised his little boy a big share of the next million quid he made. That helped.

Party night! Band playing! Dancing! Food! A cake! No expense spared! Oojilet (who thought she had a flair for disco dancing) was spinning around on the dance floor.

"Look at me! Look at me! See how my dress flares out when I spin!"

The party was in full swing with everyone blissfully unaware of the nightmare about to unfold...

Mid-spin, Oojilet clocked a face she didn't like. In the full glare of flashing disco lights, Oojilet spotted ... Monio! She got really angry!

"Monio, Monio!" she declared. "You dare to spoil my party?" She ranted. She raged.

Visitors made a run for the spare rooms to hide from the insults flying through the air. Monio didn't care. He had his share of Daddy's next million just for being there.

The problem was that as soon as her temper had flared, Oojilet couldn't stop, and no one dared to shut her up.

"It's no good," sighed Mrs Carpalot. "This will put him right off. We've wasted all this food, too!"

Monio was not put off though. In fact, he was a bit impressed. He thought, "At last, someone as spoiled as I am! What a pair we would make!"

Oojilet's insults were still blaring out of her delicate little mouth. Monio had been about to scoff a bit of party food.

He stopped.

He stared.

He grabbed a choccy eclair ... and lobbed it at the fair Oojilet.

She stopped.

She stared.

She grabbed a fairy cake and chucked it at Monio. He kept

his cool, managed to catch it in his mouth, munched, then swallowed the yummy cake. Oojilet was very steamed up at this.

"Are you aware of who I am?" she screeched.

But as she stood, hands on hips, bits of eclair stuck in her hair, she was not aware that Monio had made his next careful choice from the banquet...

Monio had a rare talent for hitting targets. A big, pink, wobbly jelly wheeled through the air and landed exactly where he intended it to land. Right in Oojilet's face.

Within a short time, all the fine fare had been thrown between the spoiled pair. No more food was left to throw. Was the fight at an end? Well, no...

Oojilet's nostrils flared. She grabbed a chair, swung it in the air and it just missed the scared Monio. What a girl! He was stunned!

It was love at first fight.

A match was declared! Monio and Oojilet were to be wed. The Montagoos' and Carpalots' riches would be shared – multi-millionaires at last!

Once upon a love match

Clare Lovehart has the name, but not the flair, for romantic matchmaking. She has set up a dating website and is struggling to match up her clients – can you help? There are no perfect matches, but who would you put together?

Don't be scared, but beware of making an awful mistake. Let me share this with you: last week, Clare teamed a Duchess who adored eating that well-known French dish, frogs' legs, with – you've got it – the Frog Prince. Need I say more?

Welcome to the *Once upon a love match* website!

"Hi, I'm Clare Lovehart. Share your dreams, and I will find your perfect match! It's all for love (plus a joining fee of £120 payable to me)."

Once upon a love match

Name: Bad Fairy

Age: 220 years old

Likes:
- Upsetting people by casting scary spells.
- Arriving at parties uninvited – I don't care!

Dislikes:
- Stuck-up princes (I tend to transform them into frogs).

WLTM (Would like to meet):

A nice, quiet young man (prepared to accept anyone under 300 years of age) who will carry my spell books, polish my magic wand and declare his undying dislike of me.

Name: Known as *Beast* for the last 5 years, but used to be known as *Handsome Beast*.

Age: 20 (ish) years old

Likes:
- My castle.
- Good food prepared by the best chefs.
- Kindness.

Dislikes:
- Visitors who pinch rare roses from my garden.
- The old woman with scary hair who cast a spell on me 5 years ago (see **Name**).
- What I see in the mirror each day – I tend to scare myself.

WLTM (Would like to meet):

Just someone who cares more about the beauty on the inside than on the outside. Someone to share my lovely lair – I mean home – and someone who dares to love a beast and wake me from this nightmare.

Name: Snow White

Age: 18 years old

Likes:

🍎 I just love everything and everybody.

🍎 Ooh – except cleaning and cooking. I had to cook for 7 men once, so now I'm not very keen.

🍎 Ooh – and except my scary stepmother (she wants to be more beautiful than me – she can't compare, poor thing).

Dislikes:

🍎 When people stare at my beautiful rose red lips and cheeks, and my hair as black as night. Anyone else might have a flare of temper at this, but I try not to show I care.

WLTM (Would like to meet):

A very handsome prince who will declare his love and always carry a spare rosy red apple for me – my favourite fare.

Name: Prince Charming

Age: 19 years old

Likes:

- ♛ A fanfare when I walk into a room.
- ♛ To glare at anyone who doesn't bow to me.
- ♛ Riding my fine white mare to a little palace I know. It's overgrown with ivy and weeds but I think I could do it up and make another spare home there.

Dislikes:

- ♛ I *hate* it when kings and queens try to ensnare me. They want to marry their daughters off to me.
- ♛ Witches and bad fairies – awful things. You never know when you might offend them and end up as a little, green slimy thing in a pond.

WLTM (Would like to meet):

A rich girl who is aware of how handsome I am and so how lucky she is.

Once upon a love match

Where you know that, one day, your prince or princess will find you...

Ask Shirley...

Letter of the week

Thursday 1st June

Dear Shirley

I really, really want a pet bird! Nothing too big, like an ostrich or a turkey, or too fancy, like a peacock or a lesser spotted whatsit. A budgie would be cool. I'd love to listen to him chirping in his cage, or whirring his wings as he sticks his darling little beak into the cookie jar. But Dad says no. Too much mess, and I should be happy playing with my dolls. Dolls, at thirteen! What can I do to change Dad's mind?

Irma

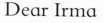

Dear Irma

What a charming letter, and what a sweet girl you are, caring so much for our little feathered friends! Sit Dad down and make him an offer: first, say you will look after the budgie and – important point – you will clean his cage, every week, until little choochie-face falls off his perch.

Shirley

PS: Birds flapping round in the kitchen are a total no-no. Tell Dad you will keep that cage closed, and he will soon be on your side!

Thursday 8th June

Dear Shirley

My problem is my brother Bert. He's a really noisy eater! At meal times, he burps and slurps so much that it makes me squirm! I felt really sick at his birthday party. Watching him eat is like watching a starving hippo with extra teeth! Please help, Shirley!

Kirsten

• •

Dear Kirsten

Thank you so much for your letter. I'm always happy to help with a problem! I will give you three tips – it's your choice.

First: Give Bert a really wide berth at meal times. Get as far away as you can – try eating your food on the roof, or on the pavement.

Second: Listen to your music at meal times – really loud. And put a blindfold on, so you don't have to look at him.

Third: Take Bert's food away, and eat it yourself. Go on – give it a whirl! (Expect to get mega-fat – and Bert will find himself on a very strict diet.)

Shirley

PS: You know, my brother gets on my nerves, too. He's got such a bad temper. I do my best to butter him up, but spending time with him is never a walk in the park. He seems to enjoy hurling abuse at me! Hmmm.

Thursday 15ᵗʰ June

Dear Shirley

I will be thirteen on my next birthday. The thing is, there's this girl I like – she's cool – but my mate just has to stick his nose in. He's always stirring it. The last straw was on Saturday when he blurted out all my feelings to her.

Kirk

• •

Dear Kirk

You and your mate are a right pair! Don't be such a wimp – be firm with him. Tell him that if he doesn't get off your case, you will dish the dirt about him to all the girls in the school. Tell him to get some R-E-S-P-E-C-T, Kirk!

Shirley

PS: And by the way, if you think your mate is a pain, you should meet my husband Bernard!

Thursday 22nd June

Dear Shirley

My teacher, Miss Burns, makes me work too hard. On a bad day, I have to work all the time. It hurts just to think about it! I hate to think what it will be like next term.

Claire

• • • • • • • • • • • • • • • • • • • •

Dear Claire

Boo-hoo, boo-hoo! Stop whining, and get over yourself! You should try working at this mag (or should I say rag) – we are on the go all day and all night! I even dream about daft letters (like yours). Is it just me – or has the editor really got it in for me?

Aaaaaaargh

On top of that, I've got a rude brother and a hopeless husband. And I've had burglars, and I've got bad feet … and I've lost my cat! You think you've got problems, but my life is a nightmare! I've got so many problems, it's all a blur! There's only one thing I can do – write to a problem page. I think it's my turn!

Shirley

Thursday 29th June

To all our readers: there is no letter of the week this week, as our beloved Shirley has been sent on gardening leave. The job was getting on top of her, and she wants to spend more time with her daffodils. Watch this space, kids!

Many happy returns
Sunburst!

It is the third birthday of Sunburst teen magazine and the latest blurb says it is undergoing a birthday makeover! We have been lurking behind the scenes to get a sneaky peek at the new look Sunburst. Be the first to check out these fab pages!

New cover!

Sunburst!

Third Birthday Special

Fashion first aid in our style surgery with 'Nurse' Fix-it!

What a makeover! Sunburst is now the first ever teen magazine for both boys *and* girls!

So what's on offer?

All the latest show-biz gossip as Blurt's lead singer, Kurt Coolman, spills the beans!

£1
Still the same price but twice as nice!

Visit the Sunburst Sports Locker and find out more about body surfing!

Free gift!
Yes, it's our birthday, but we're giving out the gifts! *Choose between:*
A funky fun purse or a fab footy calendar!

Sunburst! your letters...

What do you think of your Sunburst mag? What's fab and what could be better?

Snail mail or email – we don't mind, just as long as you write to us.

Hi Sunburst!

Love the mag but it would be even better if there were a lot more pop posters. I'm wallpapering my bedroom with them so please, please print more!

Fern Gurnhill

Hello,

I am not happy with the recipe you gave for lemon curd ice cream last month. I followed it exactly but it turned out all wrong, and the cream curdled when mixed with the lemon. Why did the recipe say 'add two tablespoons of salt'? My mates thought I was trying to murder them with poisoned food!

Anon

Dear Editor,

I had a go at the hair style shown in December's mag but I think I ended up looking a right nerd. What do other readers think? I have enclosed a pic.

Bert Hurd

Write to The Editor, Sunburst Magazine, London or email **my.letter.ed@sunburst.con**

Shirl Lee interviews

KURT COOLMAN
from
'BLURT'

*No other magazine gives **you** the chance to take over as celebrity reporter. Yes! Every month, one of our lucky readers will get to interview a superstar of their choice. First up is thirteen-year-old Shirl Lee Potter from Burton upon Trent. Shirl Lee wants to be a writer and is a mega 'Blurt' fan.*

Ace teen reporter, Shirl Lee Potter, gets the low-down from Kurt Coolman, lead singer of your fave boy band, 'Blurt'. Will he spill the beans and dish the dirt in this exclusive interview for Sunburst? Read on ...

Shirl: Hi Kurt. Your last album got to number thirty in the charts. Do you think this latest one will get to number one?

Kurt: Hi Shirl. You don't mind if I carry on eating my beans on toast, do you? I haven't had time for lunch.

Shirl: No – you keep eating. Oops! You've spilled some beans over your shirt, Kurt. What about your album? Number one?

Kurt: Oh, yes. The album. Well this is our third album and it doesn't get any better than this one. It burst into the shops yesterday and shot up to the third spot!

Shirl: Oh, that's fantastic. What is it called? Oops – those beans are flying off the fork again!

Kurt: 'Dish the Dirt', Shirl.

Shirl: What dirt, Kurt?

Kurt: That's what our new album is called.

Shirl: Right! I don't suppose you *do* want to dish the dirt on the other boys in 'Blurt', do you? Sunburst readers love a bit of gossip!

Kurt: Well, Shirl, us boy bands have a lot of fans, as you know, and one girl asked Kirk to sign a shirt in lipstick but he ... oh, just let me scoff the last bean ... umm ... er ... sorry, Shirl, I've forgotten what the punchline was going to be!

Shirl: We all know what a flirt Kirk can be, Kurt. Perhaps *you* could sign a shirt and we can give it to one of our lucky readers as a prize!

Kurt: Cool! Pass me that pen and I'll sign the shirt I've got on.

Shirl: OK, but shouldn't we wipe off those beans first?

Kurt: Good point, Shirl. Oh, I'm still hungry. Time for dessert ...

At this point, readers, Kurt's manager stopped the interview as the star couldn't speak with his mouth full of buttercream pie.

'Dish the Dirt', the latest album from 'Blurt', can be found in all good shops.

Sunburst!
The Sports Locker!

Kirsten Firl

Herman Poser

Are you a wave wimp? Do you shudder at the thought of swirling undercurrents and turbulent tides? Well, check out the beach kids who like their sport to be wet and wild! Meet British girl Kirsten Firl and German boy Herman Poser, champion body surfers!

What is body surfing?

This is an extreme sport, where surfers have to ride the waves without a surfboard! They twist, turn, and spin their back and arms while kicking (sometimes with surf flippers on), swimming and paddling as they surf and ride the waves!

"You have to be a brilliant swimmer to body surf," says Kirsten.

"Yes," adds Herman. "The stronger the wave, the better the surfing, but the danger is that you can be pulled out too far by rip tides."

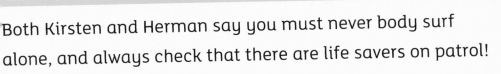

Both Kirsten and Herman say you must never body surf alone, and always check that there are life savers on patrol!

Another fab, insider's peep in The Sports Locker, but remember: **do not try this without an expert!**

Next month in **The Sports Locker**: Curling
(no, not your hair – it is a sport, no, really …)

A spell in space

How will it feel, how will it feel,
to shoot like an arrow made of steel?
Through clouds and showers of falling stars,
target – the Moon or Planet Mars.

On TV you waved farewell,
– were you scared? Who could tell?
Like a robot now, not a human being,
fixed on the places you'll be seeing.

Crowds collect at the launching place,
now the countdown into space.
Machines take over, calculate,
how much to accelerate.

3

2

1

the countdown ends. The sound of cheers.
The booster sends the rocket into the stratosphere.
Now friends and family want to clap and shout,
but hold their breath,
think (don't speak) of life and death ...

I'm here, I'm here, surrounded by night,
twinkling stars the only light.
The sun has gone and in its place,
moonless, weightless outer space.

Sealed in a space suit, I drift outside,
watching asteroids collide.
I left the ship on auto power,
I'm drifting now through a meteor shower.

I'm a star sailor, an astronaut,
I'm sailing the stars, without a thought
of drowning in this sea of dust.
Swim with the stars, I must, I must.

A peaceful place,
this outer space,
no crowds around,
no noise, no sound.

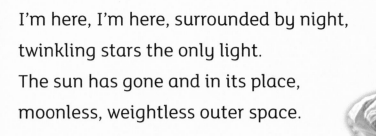

21

e to return, oxygen's low,
to the space ship I must go.
ust for a moment I'd like to snip
ord that ties me to the ship.

oted to spend eternity
ng away, no limits, free.
I think of family, friends.
noment has gone – the space spell ends.

or home, and I think I know how
ot my own place in the universe now.

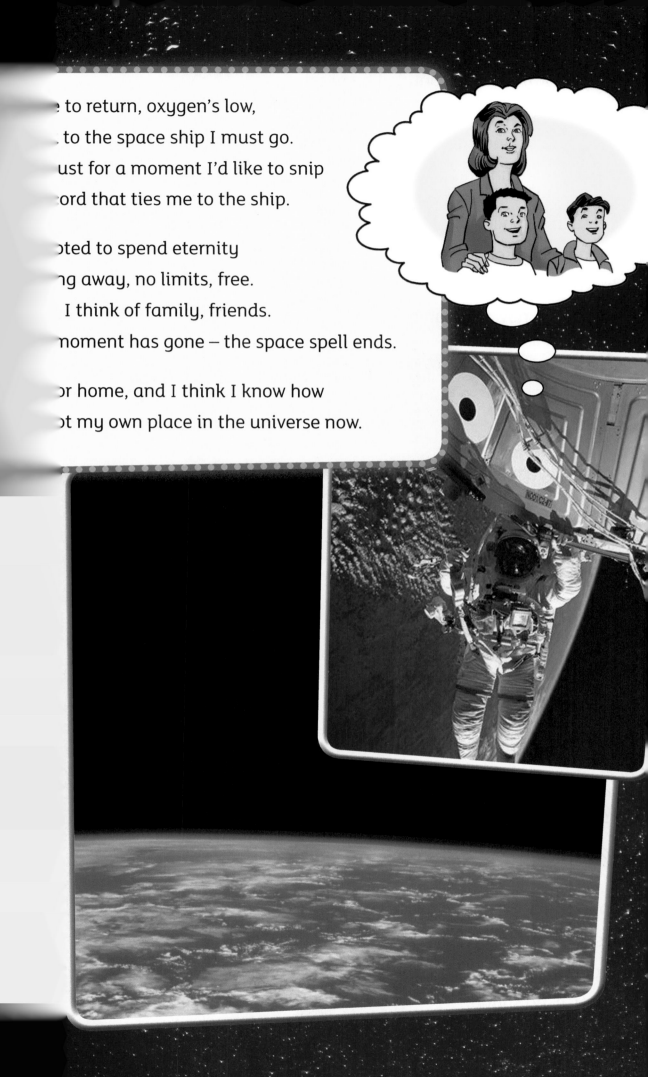

They came from outer space!

Space. Just think about it! Blows your mind, huh? So much of it, and we know so little about it.

How many stars are there? Billions, and that's just in our galaxy, the Milky Way. We've been to the Moon now, and we know a bit about the planets in our Solar System. But as for the rest...

Some of us think there are little green men out there. But why little? Why green? And why men? There have been huge numbers of sightings of UFOs (that's *unidentified flying objects* to you). Some say they have been abducted by aliens, even given medical tests by them. But experts argue about these sightings, because:

- there is no real proof
- such long-distance travel is unlikely
- sightings can be put down to dreaming
- strange lights in the sky can be put down to aircraft or tricks of light on the clouds.

Let's look at some accounts of UFOs and aliens ...

USA, 1947

Parts of a 'spacecraft' and the corpses of 'aliens' were found in the desert. Did a spaceship crash? Or was it a joke? The USA air force stated that the bits of metal came from a radar-tracking balloon ...

Italy, 1950

A man named Bruno saw a round, glowing object hovering over the ground. A ladder came down and 'aliens' clambered out – too many to count. They started to repair the 'spaceship'. Bruno shouted for help. There was a loud buzzing sound and, according to Bruno, he was knocked to the ground by a beam from a ray gun. The next day, brown patches and bits of metal were found on the grass ...

UK, 2003

A girl named Sue saw a huge, tube-shaped object hanging in the sky over her town. She watched, spellbound, as it shook itself and then took off to the south ...

Puerto Rica, 2005

This story has the wow factor! Night owl Maria looked out of the window and saw a 'flying saucer' in the sky. Then she saw a pair of 'aliens' standing in the back yard, staring right at her! They were naked, slim, and about a metre tall. They had slits for mouths and holes for nostrils.

Maria's dog crouched down and growled. The aliens made Maria go out of the house. She can't say what happened next, but hours later she found herself back in bed, in her nightgown. In the morning, Maria found a strange round mark on her hand. And the dog was ill for weeks …

How scary was that? Was Maria abducted by aliens? Do you have your doubts? How can we tell what is true? What do *you* think?

Watch this space! 2015

A planet has been found, orbiting a star. It is in the Goldilocks Zone – which means it is not too hot or too cold for water to form. Will we find life on this planet? It is 1400 light years away and it would take 26 million years to get there – a bit too far for a day trip!

Do it!

Still playing that old computer game? Boring! Now's the time to do something different – don't wait until you are old and grey. Do it! Do it straight away! Here are some things you can try.

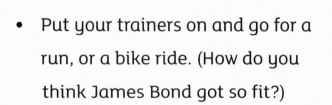

- Put your trainers on and go for a run, or a bike ride. (How do you think James Bond got so fit?)

- Go fishing, in a pond or a river. You need a rod and line, and some maggots as bait. You may catch a fish – or an old boot – or a bag full of cash!

- Change your haircut – just for fun. Go spiky, or go green! Then wait for the cutting remarks. (Get it?)

- Hook up with a penpal, and send them an e-mail – or write a letter and send it by snail mail.

- Go trainspotting. (No, not really. Just a joke!)

- Find out about first aid. With this sort of know-how, you may save a life one day.

- Train your brain with a crossword or a game of Sudoku.

- Ever thought about bungee jumping? What do you mean, too scary? Then try climbing instead. Do it!

- Go for a swim in your local pool. It's not exactly Jamaica, but it's good fun, and it doesn't matter if it rains. Don't forget your towel, snorkel and pretend shark fin.

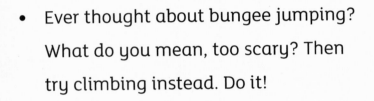

- Paint your bedroom! Important point: Check with your mum or dad first! They may not be too keen on your black and silver chain mail pattern.

- Send an e-mail to Santa Claus. No, wait – you reckon he's just for little kids, but you never know. The next time he rocks up from the North Pole in his sleigh, he may bring you sacks full of goodies!

- Have a go at weight lifting. You may be the next "World's strongest man or woman"!

- Take a flight into space! You will find out how it feels to be an astronaut, with 3 minutes of weightlessness. It will only cost you a hundred and fifty thousand quid – and it's a fail-safe way to impress your mates!

And if you're still feeling restless, have some fun at home ...

- If you have a tent, put it up in the back garden. (If your dad's a mug, don't waste your own time – get him to do it for you!) Then enjoy your den for the day!

- Bug your sister – after all, she can be a right pain! Wait until she's sorted out her vast wardrobe, and then nip into her room and unsort it. Easy! If she faints with shock, remember – you know nothing!

- Fix a target to the back wall, and see how many times you can hit it with a tennis ball. Less than eight is just sad. (This one will bug your mum if she's inside trying to watch telly, as the ball thuds against the wall again and again.)

When you've done all that, you will need a rest! Did you say, bring on the computer games?

Shark for Sale

For Sale

Shark

Loving, cuddly, great with kids.
Going cheap at just £80.
Will deliver.
Tel. 0231 1234 56789

"Eighty pounds?!" exclaimed Dad.
"Eighty pounds?!"

I waited until he'd come down off the ceiling, then put on a pained look and asked him again if I could have it. And again. And again. It never fails.

At 6 o'clock that evening, a knock came at the front door.

"You the bloke that's bought the shark?" asked a big man in a plain white rubber jacket and plain white rubber boots, standing on the doorstep.

Behind him stood two more white rubbery men, holding a big plastic bag full of water … and a baby shark.

"Is that it?" complained Dad. "Call that a shark? I've seen bigger fish down Bert's Chippy – in the kiddies' meals too!"

"It's a *baby* shark," explained a rubbery man. "Don't worry," he smiled wickedly. "It'll soon grow."

It must have weighed a fair bit, because the men were red-faced and panting with the strain by the time they got it in the paddling pool.

"I shall call him Shane," I decided. "Shane the Shark."

Luckily the box that came with Shane contained a book called *How To Look After Your Shark*. I turned to the chapter on **Feeding**.

"Sharks enjoy all seafood," I read, "but also have a taste for human meat. In case of loss of finger, arm, leg or any other body part, please seek first aid before you faint." That's odd, I thought. The advert said it was great with kids.

Next, I turned to the page on **Care**. "Sharks can make very loyal pets, but they tend to treat all strangers as enemies. Use steel gloves when training." Hmm, I thought. Cuddly?

Flicking through the book, I came to the section on **Growth**. "Baby sharks may be only 30–40 centimetres long," I read out loud, "but within 6 months can grow up to 4 metres."

"4 metres?!" wailed Dad. I could tell he was having second thoughts already. "We'll have to hire Denton Swimming Pool to keep him in!"

"Should make school swimming lessons interesting though," I remarked. "You'd soon learn to swim with Shane behind you, nibbling at your toes." I always try to look at the positive side.

Dad wouldn't have it though. "Do you think I'm brainless? How can it be loving when its first instinct is to bite your arm off? We haven't got chain mail gloves to hold it with, and it's only great with kids if you use them as bait and watch them disappear into its belly! And I paid eighty pounds for it!"

"Sharks aren't supposed to be kept as pets! It's going straight back in the morning, and if you want anything else that's going cheap, you can have a budgie!"

He likes his little jokes, does Dad.

Left alone to die –
The story of Alexander Selkirk

Alexander Selkirk was not a very easy man to get along with. In Scotland, where he was born, he upset a lot of people and did some nasty things. It got to the stage where he had two choices: stay at home and get put in jail, or run away to sea. He was only 24.

He joined a pirate ship, the *Cinque Ports*, and travelled around the world. In October 1704, the boat stopped at an uninhabited island off the coast of South America, to take on food, fresh water and stores of wood for repairs. Selkirk moaned that the boat was not fit to carry on, as there were loads of holes that made it leak. He said he would not sail on it any more, and tried to get other sailors to follow his plan and stay behind with him. Nobody did. The captain was fed up. "If you don't want to come with us, stay here then!" he roared, and set sail, leaving Selkirk alone on the beach.

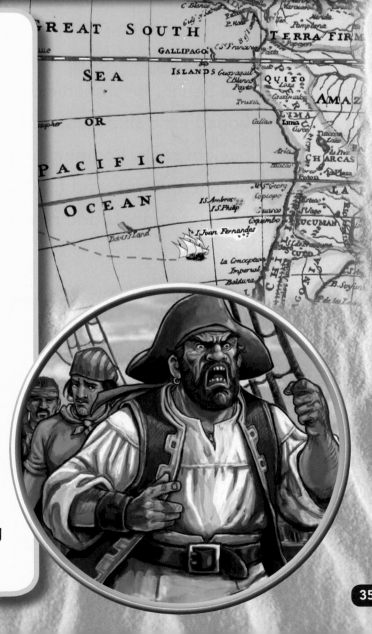

As the boat sailed away into the distance, Selkirk changed his mind. He ran up and down on the beach, shouting that he was sorry, and begging for the boat to come back, but it was hopeless. The boat had left, and he was on his own (it turned out to be a good move by Selkirk, as within a month the boat sank and most of the men sank with it!)

They had left him with just his gun, some gunpowder, his tools, a knife, clothes and food for just two or three days. He muttered crossly, reproaching himself as a fool, and moped about on the beach. He stayed close to the shore, living on shellfish, and hoped for a ship to come by, but he was driven off by an angry pack of seals. Roaming inland, he found fresh water for his parched throat, and food in the form of some beans and turnips. He hunted goats and roasted them on a fire. The goats also gave him milk to drink.

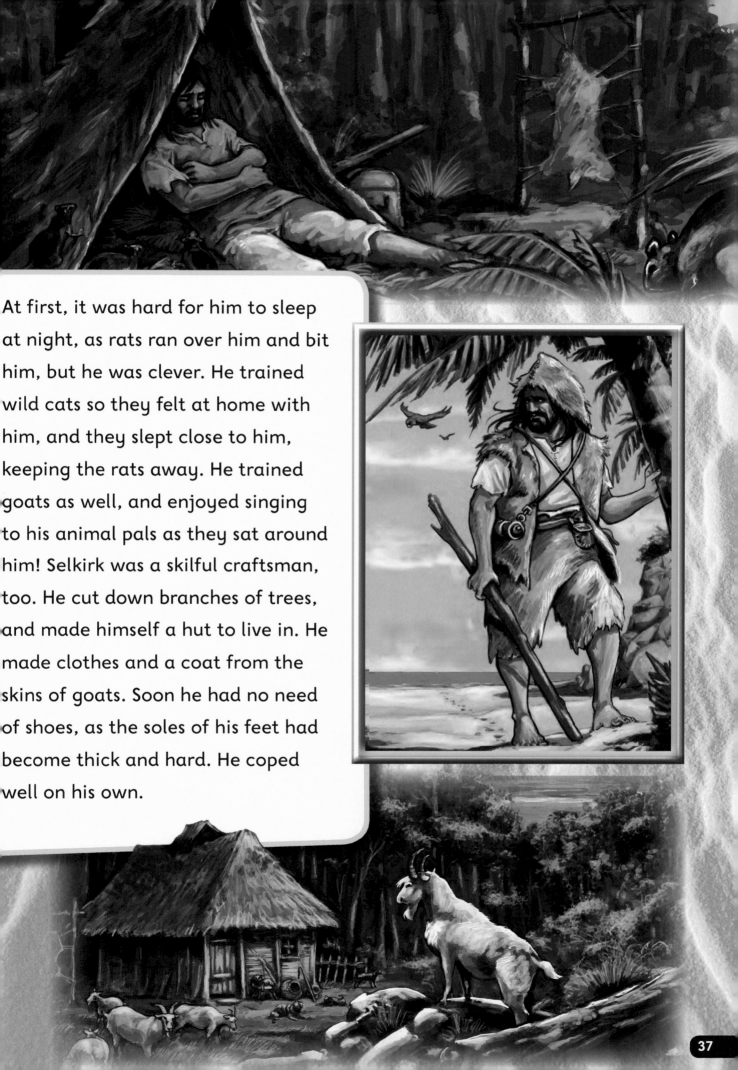

At first, it was hard for him to sleep at night, as rats ran over him and bit him, but he was clever. He trained wild cats so they felt at home with him, and they slept close to him, keeping the rats away. He trained goats as well, and enjoyed singing to his animal pals as they sat around him! Selkirk was a skilful craftsman, too. He cut down branches of trees, and made himself a hut to live in. He made clothes and a coat from the skins of goats. Soon he had no need of shoes, as the soles of his feet had become thick and hard. He coped well on his own.

He was soon very fit, so when his gunpowder ran out, he hunted on foot. One time, chasing a goat, he ran off the edge of a cliff! Luckily he landed on top of the goat, so no bones were broken, but he lay there senseless for a whole day. He kept a count of the goats he killed – 500!

He spent a lot of time sitting on a hilltop and looking out to sea, waiting for a boat to come. One day, he looked out and saw sails near the shore. At last, the moment he had hoped for! But when he ran down to approach the boat, he saw a Spanish flag. The Spanish had no love for the Scots. They shot at Selkirk, aiming to kill, but he tore off into the bushes and hid. After two days, the boat left and he was alone again.

Then, on 2nd February 1709, a British boat landed on the shore. He was saved! After four years alone on his island, he could go home again.

One day, you may read the book *Robinson Crusoe*, or see a TV series or film. It's about a man who spends a long time living alone on an island. We're quite sure that the man in that book is based on Alexander Selkirk.

Extreme survival

Are you a survivor? Do you know how to cope with outdoor life, all alone and far from home? Do this quick quiz and find out! Jot down your scores in a notebook.

1. You are going hiking on the moors. What if something goes wrong, and you need help? How can you prepare for this?

A Take a mobile phone (charged and with credit on it) and a first aid kit. Make sure someone knows where you're going.

B Take a loudspeaker so you can call for help.

C Just hope for the best! If something goes wrong, you'll cope – you're a superhero!

2. You are planning a camping trip, but it's so cold and wet that you will be frozen to the bone. Can you cope in the snow? Do you know what clothes to pack in your rucksack?

A A thick waterproof coat, shedloads of woolly socks, hiking boots and a tent!

B A very large umbrella and your kid brother's Batman cloak.

C Your bright yellow swimming trunks/costume and the pink flip-flops Granny Joan gave you.

3. You are alone at the top of a mountain, and so peckish you could eat a horse with no ketchup. But all you have is a bag of rice. What do you do?

A Light a barbie and cook the rice, with water, over the hot coals.

B Make a bow and arrow, and try to catch a goat (for toasted goat) or a toad (for toad in the hole).

C Wish you had made a packed lunch.

4. You are out exploring, but it is raining hard. What do you do?

A Find shelter in a cave or under an oak tree (unless you can see lightning).

B Make a rowing boat from twigs and a ball of string, and float along until it's over.

C Get soaking wet.

5. You are camping on the coast, and flying insects have made your nose and toes their number one dish of the day. How do you keep the beastly bugs at bay?

A Create lots of smoke around your tent with the barbie, and rub garlic on your skin (it grows in the wild).

B No use moaning – wash all your clothes in cold coffee (it just might work).

C Get the next coach home to your mum.

6. It's a cloudy evening, and you are planning a trip to visit a pal in the next town. How will you find the right road?

A Use a map.

B Rip the SatNav out of your dad's car. (Just a joke!)

C Wait until dark, and navigate by the Pole Star.

Now count up your scores.

Mainly As – congrats, you are a true survivor!

Mainly Bs – you are a crazy, have-a-go hero!

Mainly Cs – you are hopeless and should just stay indoors!

A fanfare for Monio and Oojilet (are)

Green words: *Say the sounds. Say the word.*

r<u>are</u>   sp<u>are</u>   <u>sh</u> <u>are</u>   fl<u>are</u>   gl<u>are</u>   d<u>are</u>   c<u>are</u>

Say the syllables. Say the word.

ni<u>ght</u>|m<u>are</u>   fan|f<u>are</u>   a|w<u>are</u>

Say the root word. Say the whole word.

ensn<u>are</u> → ensn<u>are</u>d   sc<u>are</u> → sc<u>are</u>d   comp<u>are</u> → comp<u>are</u>d   decl<u>are</u> → decl<u>are</u>d

Red words: lo<u>ve</u>   <u>through</u>   <u>though</u>t   <u>th</u> <u>ere</u>   couldn't   some<u>one</u>   <u>th</u> eir   every<u>one</u> <u>we</u>re   <u>wh</u>at   <u>th</u> ey   w<u>ou</u>ld   <u>wh</u>o   c<u>a</u>lled

Challenge words: d<u>ea</u> <u>th</u>   delicate   <u>how</u>   Monio   Romeo   Sh<u>a</u>kesp<u>ear</u>e families   most   ma<u>rr</u> i<u>e</u>d   disco   fly<u>ing</u>   <u>th</u> <u>ough</u>

Vocabulary check: banquet *wonderful feast for a party*   **clocked** *slang word for spotted or saw* **fanfare** *the sounding of trumpets to herald the arrival of important people*   **ensnared** *trapped* **William Shakespeare**   *a famous English writer of plays who was born in 1564*

Once upon a love match (are)

Green words: *Say the sounds. Say the word.*

<u>Cl</u>are   sp<u>are</u>   <u>sh</u> <u>are</u>   c<u>are</u>   r<u>are</u>   d<u>are</u>s   st<u>are</u>   f<u>are</u>   gl<u>are</u>   m<u>are</u>

Say the syllables. Say the word.

be|w<u>are</u>   de|<u>cl</u>are   ni<u>ght</u>|m<u>are</u>   com|p<u>are</u>   fan|f<u>are</u>   en|sn<u>are</u>   a|w<u>are</u>

Say the root word. Say the whole word.

sc<u>are</u> → sc<u>are</u>d → sc<u>ary</u>   prep<u>are</u> → prep<u>are</u>d

Red words: on<u>ce</u>   welc<u>ome</u>   stepmo<u>th</u> er   pe<u>o</u>ple   <u>th</u> ere   <u>wh</u>o   w<u>ou</u>ld anyo<u>ne</u>   w<u>a</u>lk   <u>th</u> eir

Challenge words: clients   y<u>ears</u>   y<u>ou</u> ng   wand   hands<u>ome</u>   cast le   <u>ch</u>efs woman   b<u>eau</u>ty   every<u>b</u>ody   b<u>ow</u>   d<u>augh</u>ters   find   p<u>ar</u>ties   kindne<u>ss</u> n<u>ow</u>   fav<u>ou</u>ri<u>te</u>   ivy   <u>how</u>

Vocabulary check: lair *a den, usually the home of a wild animal*   **mare** *female horse* **fare** *old-fashioned word for food*   **ensnare** *trap someone or something*

Ask Shirley ... (ur er)

Green words: *Say the sounds. Say the word.*

Bert   turn   slurps   burps   berth   nerves   term

Say the syllables. Say the word.

Thurs|day   temp|er   lett|er   butt|er   nev|er

Say the root word. Say the whole word.

blurt → blurted   eat → eater   play → playing   hurl → hurling

Red words: watching   should   where   would   there   many   walk

Challenge words: whining   beloved   dear   turkey   feathered   try   blindfold
work   over   even   only

Vocabulary check: **blurted** *talked fast and thoughtlessly*   **whining** *moaning*

Many happy returns Sunburst! (ur er)

Green words: *Say the sounds. Say the word.*

blurb   Blurt   Fern   curd   nerd   Bert   Hurd   burst   turn   surf

Say the syllables. Say the word.

re|turns   surg|er|y   su|per|star   un|der|curr|ents   Ger|man   dan|ger
re|mem|ber   cur|ling

Say the root word. Say the whole word.

surf → surfing → surfer   curdle → curdled   report → reporter   write → writer

Red words: many   thought   other   their   shouldn't   there   some
any   called   where

Challenge words: scenes   these   new   special   fashion   recipe   salt
interview   sign   turbulent   surfboard   over   behind   cover   style
now   both   we're   mind   even   wallpapering   toast   extreme   danger

Vocabulary check: **many happy returns** *happy birthday*   **lurking** *staying hidden*
snail mail *send by post*   **turbulent** *not stable or calm*   **rip tides** *strong currents*
curling *a game played on ice with flat stones*   **spill the beans** *tell someone a secret*

A spell in space (ow)

Green words: *Say the sounds. Say the word.*

how   crowds   now

Say the syllables. Say the word.

with|out   out|side   sh ow|ers   count|down   out|er

Say the root word. Say the whole word.

drown → drowning

Red words: through   here   watching   thought   their   were   who   could

Challenge words: weightless   stratosphere   breath   death   falling   machines   friends   robot   human   over   calculate   hold   only   suit   auto   meteor   moment

Vocabulary check: **accelerate** *speed up*   **eternity** *forever and ever, without end*   **stratosphere** *area of the atmosphere about 30 miles above Earth*

They came from outer space! (ou ow)

Green words: *Say the sounds. Say the word.*

now   down   brown   town   south   owl   how

Say the syllables. Say the word.

out|er   a|cc ounts   night|gown

Say the root word. Say the whole word.

sh out → sh outed   crou ch → crou ched   growl → growled

Red words: some   watch   water   they   there   many   tall

Challenge words: system   unidentified   aliens   Bruno   metre   doubts   years   flying   sky   over

Vocabulary check: abducted *take away illegally, kidnap*

accounts *reports or descriptions of an event*   **clambered** *climbed or moved in an awkward way*

Do it! (ai aigh eigh)

Green words: *Say the sounds. Say the word.*

wait   straight   eight   bait   snail   mail   train   brain   aid   paint

rains   sleigh   pain   faints

Say the syllables. Say the word.

train|ers   Jam|ai|ca   a|gain

Say the root word. Say the whole word.

cut → cutting   bore → boring   weight → weightless → weightlessness

Red words: here   some   many   watch   ball   thought

Challenge words: try   wall   minutes   world   crossword   grey   computer   find
climbing   local   woman   only   done

Vocabulary check: snail mail *send by post*   **Sudoku** *popular number quiz in newspapers*

Shark for sale (ai aigh eigh)

Green words: *Say the sounds. Say the word.*

fails   plain   strain   aid   faint   chain   mail   bait   paid   straight

Say the syllables. Say the word.

eight|y   a|gain   brain|less

Say the root word. Say the whole word.

exclaim → exclaimed   complain → complained   weigh → weighed
contain → contained

Red words: great   water   other   thought   through   though   watch   come
they   any   should   wouldn't

Challenge words: ceiling   worry   gloves   metres   toes   only   loving   front
bought   behind   human   read   months   hire   learn   disappear

Vocabulary check: pained *hurt or troubled*   **wickedly** *evilly*
loyal *firm, a constant support*

Left alone to die – The story of Alexander Selkirk (oa o)

Green words: *Say the sounds. Say the word.*

c**oa**st   b**oa**t   thr**oa**t   g**oa**t   l**oa**ds   c**oa**t

Say the syllables. Say the word.

app|r**oa**ch   h**o**pe|less   a|l**o**ne   f**o**ll|**ow**

Say the root word. Say the whole word.

m**o**pe → m**o**ped   repr**oa**ch → repr**oa**ching   r**oa**m → r**oa**ming   r**oa**st → r**oa**sted

m**oa**n → m**oa**ned

Red words: s**o**me   h**e**re   c**o**me   wat**e**r   l**o**ve   **wh**ere   **th**ere   were   w**ou**ld

any   **oth**er   pe**o**ple

Challenge words: **is**land   Crus**oe**   Febru**a**ry   w**or**ld   r**oa**red   mind   mo**v**e   fi**r**e

shoes   **wh**ole   n**ea**r   four   sure

Vocabulary check: **uninhabited** *nobody lives there*   **parched** *dry*   **reproached** *told off*

roaming *wandering*

Extreme survival (oa o)

Green words: *Say the sounds. Say the word.*

c**oa**t   cl**oa**k   J**oa**n   c**oa**ls   g**oa**t   t**oa**d   **oa**k   b**oa**t   fl**oa**t   c**oa**st

c**oa**ch   r**oa**d

Say the syllables. Say the word.

a|l**o**ne   yell|**ow**   n**o**te|b**oo**k   fr**o**|zen   a|**rr ow**   t**oa**st|ed   h**o**pe|less

Say the root word. Say the whole word.

r**ow** → r**ow**ing   s**oa**k → s**oa**king   m**oa**n → m**oa**ning

Red words: **wh**at   **wh**ere   call   bro**th**er   c**ou**ld   water   **th**eir   **sh**ould

s**o**me**o**ne   ba**ll**

Challenge words: **s**ure   super**h**ero   cold   wa**sh**   t**oe**s   **s**urvival   try   find   w**or**k

Vocabulary check: **shedloads** *a large amount*   **Pole Star** *a bright star used to guide travellers*